C000173803

SMILE...
MIRACLES WILL HAPPEN!

FIRST PUBLISHED IN THE UNITED KINGDOM
IN 2008 BY THE CREATIVE DREAM COMPANY,
138 UPPER STREET, LONDON, N1 1QP

PRINTED AND BOUND IN THE UNITED
KINGDOM BY BIDDLES LTD, KINGS LYNN,
NORFOLK

ISBN 978-0-9559197-0-1

WRITTEN AND ILLUSTRATED
BY BRIAN I. DAVIS
DESIGN BY KATRIN FUERNSCHUSS

To: JILL   23.12.13

YOU'RE AMAZING!!

DO SOMETHING
AMAZING IN
2014!!
2015
2016... ETC!!

bid.

TO
MY MUM...
AND ALL THE OTHER
ANGELS IN MY LIFE

ESPECIALLY
ZÖE, ADAM, ZACHARI
et FRÉDÉRIQUE

HOW IT STARTED...

ANGELS HAVE OFTEN COME
INTO MY LIFE. I MET MY
WIFE THROUGH THEM...
BUT THAT'S ANOTHER STORY*
[*GIVE ME A SIGN, HOLISTIC LONDON, 1998]
    THIS YEAR I RECEIVED
THE LETTER FROM THE BANK
EVERYONE DREADS...
REPOSSESSION. I BURST
OUT CRYING, SWALLOWED
HARD AND TRIED NOT TO PANIC
... BUT IT WAS IMPOSSIBLE.
    FORTUNATELY SOME TIME
AGO I HAD CREATED A
BOX OF ANGEL CARDS TO
SUPPORT ME AT TIMES
LIKE THESE. I DREW OUT
ONE, BUT THREE CAME OUT...

♥ LIVE YOUR DREAM
♥ THINK
♥ TEAM UP

I FELT THE ANGELS WERE
LAUGHING AS MY WIFE SAID
I WAS RUNNING THE

CREATIVE NIGHTMARE COMPANY

AS THE DEBTS WERE SO BAD!
RATHER THAN THE

CREATIVE DREAM COMPANY

I'D FORMED A DECADE AGO
TO HELP PEOPLE MAKE THEIR
CREATIVE DREAMS COME
TRUE~HOWEVER WILD!!

SO I LOOKED AT THESE
THREE LITTLE CARDS AND
DREW AN ANGEL ON MY DIARY
... EVERYDAY SINCE I HAVE
DRAWN ONE OR MORE ...
AND MIRACLES HAVE BEGUN
HAPPENING.
FRIENDS AND STRANGERS
OPEN THEIR HEARTS
AND SAY THE ANGELS HAVE
GIVEN THEM A LIFT...
I HOPE THIS TASTE OF
ANGEL DELIGHTS
WILL DO THE SAME FOR YOU.
NOTE: WITHIN 24 HOURS OF THOSE
CARDS I RECEIVED 3 OFFERS FOR
MY FLAT AND AN IMMEDIATE BUYER
AND AM USING PART OF THE PROCEEDS
TO PUBLISH THIS BOOK AND SPREAD...

...EVERY DAY ON www.myangeladay.com

PICK A CARD

SHIFT HAPPENS!

SURVIVAL
REQUIRES
MORE THAN
FITNESS...

SPARKLE

CONTROL YOUR LIFE
DON'T LET LIFE CONTROL
YOU

ASK FOR
HELP!

TEARS LEAVE SPACE
FOR THE JOY
TO ENTER

JOIN THE
HUG CLUB

LIVING SIMPLE
CAN BE REALLY
COMPLICATED

FORGIVE
SOMEONE
?
GIVE THEM
A RING _NOW_...

IT'S A
REVELATION!

LIVE WITH
PASSION

FORGIVE
YOURSELF

NOBODY ELSE
CAN BE OR DO
WHAT YOU DO...
WOW!

SUCCESS IS A
STATE OF MIND...
YOURS!

NEGATIVITY
STINKS

HAPPINESS CAN
FIND YOU
ANYWHERE

NOBODY SUCCEEDS
ALL THE TIME...
FORTUNATELY
NOBODY FAILS
ALL THE TIME
EITHER!

DON'T BE AFRAID
TO CRY

THERE IS ONLY
ONE CREDIT RATING
THAT MATTERS...
HOW YOU RATE
YOURSELF!

LIVE
LIGHT

UNLOCK YOUR
POWER

ANOTHER DAY...
ANOTHER CROISSANT!

INSPIRATION OFTEN
COMES OUT OF
DESPERATION

THINK

TEAM UP

EVEN OUR MISTAKES
HAVE A PURPOSE

NOW IS THE TIME
TO HAVE THE TIME OF YOUR LIFE

DARE TO BE
DIFFERENT

TRUST
YOURSELF

RELEASE YOURSELF

JUMP FOR JOY!

LIFE SHOULD BE AS
GOOD AS CHOCOLATE

OFTEN WE LEARN MORE
FROM OUR MISTAKES
THAN OUR SUCCESSES!

THE ONLY THING
I CAN'T RESIST IS
TEMPTATION!

FOCUS 10% ON THE PROBLEM
AND 90% ON THE SOLUTION

PLAY WITH
POSSIBILITIES!

DON'T LISTEN TO
YOUR MOTHER...
TALK TO STRANGERS!

WORK WITH WHAT
YOU HAVE ...

SURROUND YOURSELF
WITH POSITIVE PEOPLE

SUCCESS IS TIMELESS

GO WITH ANGELS
MEET WITH ANGELS
WALK WITH ANGELS
WORK WITH ANGELS
ANGELS ON YOUR BODY
AND
COME HOME
WITH ANGELS"

pid.

The R. von Breslay

WHAT'S THE
ALTERNATIVE?

LOVE LEARNING...

LEARN LOVING!

ACT NOW!

FIT BODY...
FIT MIND

IF YOU BELIEVE IN MONSTERS
∘∘∘ THERE BE MONSTERS

RELEASE YOURSELF

FREE YOURSELF...

TODAY IS A GIFT
THAT'S WHY IT'S CALLED
... THE PRESENT

PURSUE YOUR
VISION

HAVE GREAT EXPECTATIONS

GOOD THINGS HAPPEN
WHEN YOU LEAST EXPECT!

GROW UP
NOT DOWN!

SAVE AND PROSPER

BE AWARE...

ANTICIPATE CHANGE

DECLARE
INDEPENDENCE

NO SUCH WORD AS 'CAN'T'...
YOU <u>CAN</u> AND YOU MUST!

SLEEP ON IT

YESTERDAY
IS HISTORY

TOMORROW
IS MYSTERY...

SO LIVE IN THE *NOW!*

SET BIG TARGETS

IF THEY WERE TO FILM
YOUR STORY WHO
WOULD IT STAR?

LIFE IS LIKE A SPRING...
 THE HARDER YOU
 PUSH IT DOWN...
THE HIGHER IT BOUNCES!

HAVE FAITH

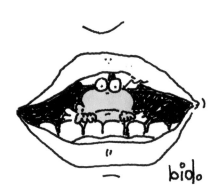

WALK YOUR TALK

WELCOME
CHALLENGE

ANY EXCUSE
FOR A PARTY

FOCUS

WE DON'T SELL ANGELS
WE SHARE THEM

THIS IS ALL AN ILLUSION...
MAKE IT A BRILLIANT ONE

CHILL ...
YOU DESERVE IT

YOU'RE BEAUTIFUL

TODAY I SAW A FEATHER
IT WAS A BIT
   GREY AND MANKY...
BUT EVEN MANKY
   BIRDS FLY!

FEAR EATS THE SOUL...
SO CHANGE YOUR
PERCEPTION!

WARNING:
NEGATIVITY CAN RUIN
YOUR HEALTH

BREAK OUT

NO REGRETS

GET MOVING

MIRACLES HAPPEN...
REACH FOR
THE STARS!

I LOVE YOU

INVEST
IN
YOURSELF

THIS IS THE BEGINNING...

INSPIRATIONS

LIFE With PICASSO

SPIKE Milligan PUCKOON

James Thurber

Carlos Castaneda Tales of Power

THICH NHAT HANH MIND...

ROBERT CRUMB

PAULO COELHO THE PILLS

CHUCK SPEZZANO PhD
HAPPINESS IS THE BEST REVENGE

WOODY ALLEN SIDE EFFECTS

TONY ROBBINS

DR SEUSS   TEN TALES

IRVIN D. YALOM Love's Executioner

ILLUSTRATED BY kido

... AND MANY MORE

+ PREMIER FOODS INTL ... I'M SURE THEIR DESSERT IS DELICIOUS ... BUT I HAVEN'T TASTED IT YET!!

NOTES

LOOK OUT FOR
FEATHERS...
IT MEANS YOU'RE
GOING TO FLY!

www.myangeladay.com